SAMPSON
and
The WIZARD

CALEB JONES

©Copyright 2016 DCS International LLC and Caleb Jones
5813 NE 63rd St. #127
Vancouver, WA 98661
USA
www.calebjones.com

TABLE OF CONTENTS

Introduction 5
Chapter 1 7
Chapter 2 11
    Tenet One 16
    Tenet Two 24
Chapter 3 27
    Tenet Three 31
    Tenet Four 40
    Tenet Five 46
Chapter 4 49
    Tenet Six 58
    Tenet Seven 61
Chapter 5 65
    Tenet Eight 72
Chapter 6 75
    Tenet Nine 79
About the Author 85

INTRODUCTION

It took me my entire life to write this book.

When I was 18 years old, I sat down and wrote a list of goals that I wanted to hit by age 28. During the next ten years I worked very hard, did a lot of things right, and a lot of things wrong. By my late twenties when the dust had settled, I had indeed hit all of my life goals.

That's when I began writing this book. My goal was to encapsulate everything I had learned into a simple, short book that could be quickly read and understood. I outlined it and wrote about 70% of it. Then life, as it so often does, took some odd turns. My attention had to be focused elsewhere and I left the book unfinished.

Ten years went by. During that time I experienced many wonderful things that were beyond even the imagination of that ambitious 18 year-old kid so many years ago. Most of these things were good, beyond my wildest dreams. Some were bad. All of them made me grow.

One day, I remembered this book. I went through my old computer files, dug it out and read it. While I mostly still agreed with its core concepts, it was rough around the edges. The principles taught in the book were accurate but incomplete. Using the new knowledge and experience I had, I sanded off the edges of the book, polished it, redirected it a little, and made it just right.

For several years I offered it for free as a PDF download. I asked for and received feedback from many readers. I updated it, had several professional editors and proofreaders clean up the copy, and now you have in your hands the final version, the version it was always meant to be.

The concepts in this book can be used to accomplish success in any area of life. Business, money, career, fitness, relationships, anything. These principles are universal and they work. I know, because I've used them many times to great effect.

If you use these concepts to accomplish positive changes in your life, my time and effort in writing this book was worthwhile.

I have outlined several sequels to this book, and will publish those if this book sells enough copies. So, if you find this book valuable, spread the word...and Sampson may return.

Until next time.

CALEB JONES
APRIL, 2016

Chapter One

The young man wiped his brow once more as he returned to working the deer hide with his wooden paddle, pressing the buckskin to squeeze out all moisture as thoroughly as possible. Had his father, the village leatherworker, been looking over his shoulder, he might scold him for working the paddle too quickly or too forcefully. The smell of deer, moose and cow hides arrayed all about the tanner's outdoor work area was overpowering, but the boy was quite used to the stench, having been around it his entire life.

"Sampson!" called a gruff voice behind him. Sampson turned to see his father, a stocky muscular man with forearms and thighs like tree trunks.

"I know, I know", responded the young man, "I have three more buck hides to get on the stretchers, then I start on the moose tomorrow."

"No, I am not worried about the moose," said his father, shaking his head. Sampson was surprised. He had been hearing news of the war in the distant south of the kingdom, and the demand for the thicker moose leather, used for the leather armor of the king's archers, was on the wax.

"Drop the paddle for the moment and come inside," his father continued in an uncharacteristically calm voice, "I have something to discuss with you."

Sampson frowned as he dropped the paddle in the tool bucket. He was in trouble again - he knew it. He glanced up at the afternoon sun before issuing one last sigh and followed his father into the house.

"I told you," Sampson began before his father even started speaking, "I would replace the sow hide from the other day with my own money."

His father smiled and bent back slightly on his wooden chair. "I am not worried about the sow hide either," he said quietly.

"Then what?" Sampson asked, growing more nervous by the minute.

"I know you do not think well of my profession," his father said. Sampson started to say something, but his father stopped him with an upraised hand. "I say this with no malice," he continued, "for it is every father's desire to see his son follow in his path, and if his son was made for a different road, then so be it. I have accepted this. I know that you have never had any desire to grow to become a master leatherworker. So, I am hereby telling you now, Sampson my son, that you are no longer beholden to me to choose your profession in life, that you are free to be whatever you choose. As long as your chosen path is not one that involves crime, deceit or dishonor, you have my blessing to do what you will."

Sampson sat aghast. His father had been a tanner since he was a small child, as was his father before him. Most of the other young men in his village of about Sampson's age, being in their late teens and early twenties, were also trained, groomed and expected to be exactly what their fathers were. It was so with the blacksmith's son, the farmer's son, the tailor's son, and it was so with Sampson. At least until now.

"Thank you, father," Sampson replied after a moment, "I know how hard that is for you to say."

"Nay," said his father, "It was hard only in the beginning. Very soon, you will be a man, your own man, and you will need to find your own way. It will be harder for you than the others, since they have their lives completely laid out before them by others. You however, have a blank slate. The responsibility is not a small one. So tell me, what is it you wish to do with your life?"

At this question, Sampson sat upright, suddenly alive with energy. His mouth was a gaping smile and his eyes flashed with white fire. "I want to amass a fortune in gold and silver," he said dreamily, "I want a castle on a high green hill, filled men-at-arms adorned in golden plate armor that sparkles in the sunlight. In time, I might even want my own kingdom, but not a kingdom like most, where everyone obeys the king's commands like slaves, but one where men are truly free to live their lives how and where they wish." A slow grimace formed on his father's face as he spoke, but so enraptured by his own fantasy, Sampson did not notice and continued.

"And I wish to be married to a woman whose skin is like milk, whose hair is like spun platinum, and whose eyes are as deep as the ocean. I wish to walk out on one of the high towers of my castle, overlooking the sea, and take her in my arms. And children! I want children! But, I do not want children who have to grow up always wanting, and never having. I want children who are fulfilled, and wise. I would have the wisest scholars in the realms come to teach and train them personally, so that they may grow to achieve true joy instead of the monotonous, dreary living that most must endure."

His father leaned forward and pointed an angry finger. "I said I would support you in what you wish to do as a man," he boomed, "but that insane thinking will get you nowhere, boy, except the ditch, if you are lucky, or the king's dungeons if you are not! Gods! I thought you might have come up with something as daft and fanciful as all that dung you just spouted! I have accepted that you will never become a leatherworking man, but I shall not see you go to the gallows in pursuit of some fairy tale!"

At that, Sampson's father stood up and stormed off. Sampson bolted out of his own chair when he realized that his father's destination was Sampson's own bedroom.

"What are you doing?" Sampson asked, as his father proceeded to empty his dresser of all its contents.

"You are leaving," his father said simply.

"What?" Sampson cried.

"Take these clothes and pack what you need," his father proceeded, "You will be gone for several months at least."

"What are you talking about?" Sampson said, "Where am I going?"

"I was hoping it would not come to this," his father said, finishing off that last drawer, "but you are my son, and I will do what is right for you even if your mother and I do not wish it in our hearts. You are going to spend the next several months under the tutelage of the wisest man I know, if not the most…conventional. You are going to stay with the Archmage. I have already arranged it."

Sampson's head was swimming. The Archmage! The greatest, wisest and most powerful wizard in the kingdom…some said in all the kingdoms! Sampson had only heard tales of the wizard's exploits, and the Archmage was as mythical a creature to the young man as a unicorn.

"The Archmage?" Sampson blurted out, "But…but how do you know him? Why would he agree to see a nobody like me? Certainly he must have better things to do! And…and…I do not wish to become a wizard!"

"At least on that we agree!" roared his father, "Goodness, that is the last thing you should want to be! If I had my way, you would already be on your way to the conscription office to become a soldier in the king's army! Perhaps there you would get your brain stuffed back in your head! But to be beaten with stick or sword is not what you need. Gods knows I could do that myself! No, what you need is wisdom, knowledge and good horse sense. And, although nothing would make me happier than to have all the world's wizards fall off the edge of the earth and take all of their cursed magic with them, I do believe that the Archmage is the best person I know to set you back on the path of wisdom."

"But…" Sampson began.

"No buts!" his father snapped. "The decision has already been made. Your mother will give you a large sack from the barn to pack your things, and you are off at first light in the morning."

Sampson could do nothing but gape at the small pile of clothes on his bed.

Chapter Two

Sampson stood at the base of the wizard's tower like an ant gazing up a redwood tree. The tower was cylindrical and huge, but not particularly spectacular to look at. It was made of a simple gray stone, very few windows, and one large wooden door. Sampson dropped his sack and knocked. The young man nearly jumped out of his skin when a voice spoke to him from nowhere.

"Who is it?"

The voice had come from no direction Sampson could discern. He whipped around, scanning the area. No one could be seen.

"I said, who is it?" the crotchety voice came again.

"My name is Sampson," the young man responded, directing his voice upwards towards the tower, "My father said…"

"Yes, yes, yes," the voice said again, "Come in. Quickly now."

The door opened before Sampson, leading into a wide hallway. Sampson could still see no one. Hoisting his sack, he slowly entered. He jumped again when the door slammed shut behind him, completely on its own.

"Please do not dawdle," the irritable voice came again, "Down the hall and to the right. Through the door and up the stairs. Quickly now."

Sampson shook his head and followed the instructions. He found himself in a large room with one rectangular table in the center rimmed with twelve simple chairs. The only door to the room was the one he had entered from. All was as quiet as a tomb.

"Hello?" he said, peering about the room this way and that.

"Hello?" the old voice came, "Why are you greeting me again? You have already done it."

Sampson turned back to the table to see a man sitting there who was not there before. He was an old man, very old, judging by his white hair and long beard that crept all the way down to his knees. He wore a dark green robe, very plain and quite uncomfortable looking. Most of the man's face was covered by his beard, but Sampson could see that despite his aged appearance, the man's eyes were sparkling, youthful and alive with power. Sampson glanced at the door and then back to the old man.

"How did you…" Sampson began.

"Not on today's agenda," the man interrupted, "Please sit down. Any chair will do."

Sampson sat down, several chairs away from the old man who sat at the head of the table. He placed his sack on the table, at which the man raised a hairy eyebrow.

"What is in there?" the old man asked.

"My clothes, and other personals, sir," Sampson replied, trying to be polite.

"Ah," the old man said. He folded his fingers and regarded the young man. Several moments went by and Sampson grew quite uncomfortable.

"Well?" Sampson asked, more to break the silence than anything.

"Well what?" the man replied, "'Well?' is not a complete question, and useless words are a sign of a chaotic mind."

Sampson blushed and tried to think of something to say.

"Then let me ask you a complete question," said the man, "What are you thinking right now?" When Sampson hesitated, the man continued with a small smile, "Please, be honest. No answer you give will offend or anger me."

"I was thinking," Sampson said after a moment, "that you told me to be quick and hustle up to this room, as if something important were happening and time was of the essence. Then when I arrive, you waste time by just sitting and staring at me."

"Interesting," said the old man, "Do you realize the number of inaccurate assumptions you make in that one statement alone?"

"No."

"I thought not. First you assume that nothing important is happening, when in point of fact something very important is occurring. Then you assume that time is not of the essence, when, in fact, time is the very essence of the universe. Every moment is as precious as any diamond mined from beneath the mountains. Then you proceed to assume that my observations of you are a waste of time, when, in fact, observing a thing to enhance one's knowledge applicable to one's objectives is never, ever, a waste of time."

"Then you must be the Archmage, the man my father sent me to see."

"Must I? No, I must not. Such a thing would denote that I had no choice in the matter. But I am nonetheless. Yes."

"So, when do we begin?"

"Begin? We have already begun. We began the moment you unceremoniously landed at my doorstep."

"And…when does it end?" At that the Archmage smiled, a surprisingly warmer smile than Sampson believed the old wizard capable.

"It never ends. Your acquisition of knowledge and experience should never end, not while you draw air into your lungs. But, we shall discuss that later. In the meantime, you are to unpack your belongings in your room, back downstairs and straight ahead, past the hall in which you entered. I assume you know how to read and write."

"Yes, sir," Sampson replied, quite proud of the fact he was one of the few young men in his village who possessed such a skill.

"Good," the Archmage said, "You will find pen and parchment in your room. You are to bring it with you when you see me again, which will be tomorrow morning, and every subsequent time you see me. Tonight, you will write out, in precise detail, everything you want in your life. And make sure you are precise! Do not put anything to paper that you do not wish! Pretend that tomorrow I am going to impart on you a magic wand that with a simple wave, will give you everything you write down tonight, exactly as you have written it, but no more."

"Are you going to give me such a wand?" Sampson asked wide-eyed.

The old wizard shook his head slowly and said "Even if such a wand existed, even if it were in my power to create such an item, I would never give to you, or anyone else such a thing. For what then, would be the reason for life itself?"

Sampson's eyes rolled sideways, quite confused.

"Yes," Archmage said, "I see we have quite some work to do."

The next morning, Sampson met the Archmage in the wizard's expansive library. In this room, all four walls were lined with books of every size and color imaginable, neatly arranged in bookshelves that reached all the way into the room's towering ceiling. Sampson noticed that there was no ladder. His musings were answered when he saw the old wizard sitting at a desk with several books wide open and floating in midair about him.

"Punctual", the Archmage said, not looking up, "Good. Sit."

Sampson seated himself in the chair opposite the old man. "I did as you asked," he said, "I wrote out everything I want, in detail. It was quite a chore… more work than I expected."

"All worthwhile things are," said the wizard. As the man turned to regard the boy, all of the floating books quietly closed themselves, glided up to their respective places in the bookshelves and inserted themselves back where they belonged. Sampson shook his head in wonder. It would take time to get used to seeing things like this.

"Would you like to see it?" Sampson asked sheepishly, holding the parchments out to the wizard. The Archmage gave the boy a curious expression.

"Why would I want to see it?" he asked, "I said write down the things in life you want, not the things in life I want."

"But, you asked me to write it all down. So I assumed…"

"There you go assuming again. A habit of yours we shall endeavor to break. Surely you see the value in putting to paper your desires for your life?"

"Well, of course," said Sampson, "Writing down your objectives, your goals, is the primary method to get what you want. I know this. I have read it in books. But I also thought that you would want to see it."

"I gave you the exercise for you, not for me. And I already knew that you understood that putting your objectives down to paper was a necessary first step to accomplish anything. I believe many people know this. But the exercise is not yet complete. Are you sure that what you have written is what will make you happy?"

"Why, of course," said Sampson, annoyed at the silly question.

"Are you quite sure?" the wizard asked again, "Because that, of course, is your primary objective."

"What is?" Sampson asked.

"Write what I am about to say on a new piece of parchment," the wizard said, and Sampson did so. He wrote:

Tenet One

Your primary objective is to accomplish that which will make you the happiest in the long term. If you are unaware of what this is, find out.

"Excuse me, sir," said Sampson looking at his paper, "But that is obvious."

"Is it?" asked the wizard, "If it is so obvious as you say, why is it that most people never do it? Did you know there are many people years older than you, men and women in their forties, fifties, and even older, who have never determined exactly what would make them happy in their lives? They simply go to school, then go to a profession that they simply "end up" in. Then, they marry a person that they meet completely by chance. Then, they have children. Not by any pre-described plan or desire, mind you, they just do precisely that, 'have children'. Why? Because everyone else 'has children'. And they keep 'having children' until they believe they can not afford anymore, even though they usually are unable to afford the first child, since they did not plan accordingly. And all the while, they have never determined if doing all of these things would truly make them happy in the long-term."

"But, that is simply not true," Sampson responded, "I know many of my friends who have said 'I want to be a soldier in the king's army when I become a man', or 'I want to be a seafarer when I become of age', or other such things."

"Indeed. Are they saying these things because they want them? Or because they *think* they want them? Or because they appear to be enjoyable with the limited amount of knowledge they possess? Or because their parents want it for them? Or because their friends want the same things? Or because an attractive young girl once told them she 'likes soldiers'? No. None of these people have given true, quiet thought to whether these things will truly make them happy. These are the people who grow to adulthood only to despondently toil at a profession for one reason only - to put food on the table for the family. There is little or no happiness. There is only obligation."

"But why?" Sampson asked, thinking of the many boys and girls in his village who would grow up to simply become as their parents were, "Why do people come to have lives such as this?"

"Very simple," responded the wizard, "Because they have never taken the time to sit down quietly and think about it."

Sampson sat in thought, and though he wanted to deny it, the trueness of the man's words rung deep within him.

"You are one of the lucky few," the Archmage said, "You already know, at a reasonably young age, what will make you happy. Some people are blessed in this area. They know in their teens or early twenties precisely they want to do with their lives, what they were meant to do. But, most people do not have this blessing. For them, their primary objective should not be dictated by their parents, teachers, masters or friends. It is instead to find out what it is that will make them happy for the long term in their life."

"What do you mean, it 'should not be dictated by their teachers and masters?'" Sampson asked.

"Tell me - what is it your parents, teachers, mentors, masters, village elders, and other grown men and women tell you and others of your age?"

"They tell us to learn skills," said Sampson, thinking hard, "They tell us to get schooling, and get good marks. Then to work, and gain knowledge in, our professions. To make sure we earn enough coin to pay for our families."

"Wonderful sounding advice, all of which has absolutely nothing to do with what will make them happy. They follow that advice, the advice of schooling and profession, and become one of those lost, dissatisfied men and women I described earlier."

"But surely people need to be schooled and learned in a craft, do they not? Do you want people to become talentless idiots, to just wander off in pursuit of foolish self-indulgence?"

"Of course not! Do not be a fool!" the old man barked, "Never once have I said that schooling or learning a trade is not of value! Do you not see all of the tomes I have within this library? Schooling and tradesmanship is of the utmost importance!"

"But...", Sampson began confused.

"But these things are of value only when that person has determined what will make him happy first. Then, he puts forth the effort in the acquisition of knowledge to best provide him what he wants the quickest. But simply going to school or learning a trade without first *precisely* determining what it is that will make you happy is insanity of the highest order."

"But you said that most people, especially young people, do not yet truly know what will make them happy. What should they do then? Surely they cannot just amble around, not learning and not growing, while they determine what it is that they want."

"That is correct. Just because they are unaware of what will make them truly happy does not mean that time does not still flow or that life does not continue.

They must still receive schooling or work in their profession to provide income for themselves, but they must do so with their primary objective in mind! And if they are unaware of what will make them happy, their primary objective is what?"

"Ah," said Sampson, understanding, "their primary objective is to determine what will make them happy, and use their current schooling, professional skills and work to make this determination as quickly as possible."

"Good," said the old man, "you are not entirely dim. That at least is a small comfort."

Sampson began to smile and then stopped while he tried to determine whether or not he had just been complimented.

"But, here is something my father would say," Sampson continued after a moment, "and I would actually agree with him if he were to say it - happiness alone cannot be a goal. There are many things that might make one happy but may also be harmful or foolish. What if what made me happy was that I drank ale at the local tavern for ten hours per day? Or what if pillaging and killing made me happy, as the pirates of the eastern sea are said to do? What then?"

The old wizard's eyes narrowed and a tiny curl came to his lips. "Young Sampson," he said, "now you are thinking. Now your mind is engaged. Now we are truly involved in the process of creation. Good. To answer your question! Did you not read what I had you write? What is the primary objective? Note that I did not say to determine simply what would make you happy, but what would make you happy in the long term. Do you honestly believe that indulging in fermented drink would make anyone truly happy in their heart of hearts over the long haul of their entire life?"

Sampson, recalling several drunks in his own village, already knew the answer to that question.

"Or," the wizard continued, "what about not working, not earning coin, and simply amusing yourself in recreational activities day in and day out? Would that make you happy in the long term? In the short term, certainly! But what about over the long years? Let us take your extreme example of the pirate. Let us assume that you have a diseased mind, and the killing of innocents or theft of others' property makes you happy, at least in the short term. Do you believe that men such as this are truly and honestly happy throughout the entirety of their lives? Even if they do actually manage to avoid capture and incarceration by the authorities? Logic and universal law would dictate otherwise. There are many things in this life that make people happy in the short term, for an hour, for a day, perhaps even for a week or a month. But, over a longer period of time, these same things make people equally miserable. As I said, time is the essence of the universe. Time must be applied to all concepts to prove their validity, and happiness is no exception."

"Then I shall challenge you again," said Sampson, "Let us assume that I want to amass great wealth, for I do! Let us suppose that I am certain that great wealth will make me happy, as well as make my family happy. But, let us then suppose that I achieve my wealth through being deceitful to others. Then I have my wealth, for the rest of my life, for the long term and I am happy. Are you saying that virtues such as honesty, integrity, kindness and love for one's fellow man mean nothing if I am happy?"

"You are quickly becoming the Lord of Assumptions," the Archmage responded, "You assume that if you acquired your wealth through deceit or force that you will still be happy. That then brings us to something I had not planned on enumerating until later in your training. But, alas, you have proved slightly less moronic than I had assumed.

"Though many do not acknowledge this fact, it is simply not possible to be an evil person, or to regularly engage in evil acts, and be happy in the long term at the same time. That is no more possible in the reality we live in than it is for the sun to set in the north or for rain to fall upwards out of the ocean and into the sky. Those who, as you have stated, have amassed great wealth, fame, or power, through evil means are not truly happy. Even if they appear happy to others when in public, or even if their affluent trappings engender the envy of others, these people, when they are alone with themselves, are anything but happy. Some are the most privately miserable people in the world. Many have charred wrecks in the form of failed marriages, unhealthy bodies, distressed children, legal entanglements, and a host of other troubles. No, these are not happy people. That is not to say that great wealth causes unhappiness. Certainly not! It is to say that amassing great wealth, or anything else worthy, through the use of evil acts will not bring long term happiness. It simply cannot be any other way.

"And I shall say something else," continued the Wizard, "there are those who believe and preach that somehow happiness is wrong. There are many philosophies that uphold this. Some say it is wrong to be happy when others in the world are unhappy. That it is wrong to be wealthy, or have a Herculean physique, or own nice things, because it is simply not fair to others who do not have these things. This is, of course, quite untrue. If you are in the process of acquiring anything that makes you happy in the long term, regardless of what that is, provided you are not engaging in evil acts to acquire it, you are doing the world a great service, not a sin.

"There are still others who hold a quite different stance. They believe that if happiness is pursued with vigor, then you are not pious, not holy, and that whatever god or gods they worship will look down upon you. Unless these are evil gods, no god could possibly look with disfavor if you are engaged in pursuit of happiness through no evil deeds. These views are usually held by those who feel some measure of guilt when they see truly happy people. You will meet both kinds of these people in abundance as you live and grow in the world. Be polite, but pay them no mind."

"Well," Sampson said, "I hate to simplify things, but if I do nothing but seek my own happiness, is that not a little greedy? What about, for example, giving alms to the poor? Or lending a kind hand to those in your family?"

"Ah, we have already touched on this," said the Archmage, "but I will get very specific with you now. If you are married to a woman whom you love, what possible motivation would you have to be kind to her?"

"Because she is my wife, and I love her," Sampson said simply. The old wizard frowned.

"Try a little harder than that," the old man said in a low voice.

"Well," said Sampson, "If I truly do love her, I would want to do nice things for her..."

"Yes!" said the old man, "But why?"

"Because it would make her feel good."

"So? Why do you care how she feels?"

"Because, if she feels good, I feel good!" Sampson burst out.

"Of course!" the old man cried, slapping his knee, "So what you are saying is that it brings *you* happiness to bring happiness to your wife. Therefore, if your goal is to acquire happiness, it is in your best interest to be kind to your wife, always. The same goes for your children, your neighbors, and everyone else you come into contact with on a regular basis. Because, as you said, the happier they are, the happier you are. This is nothing new. Surely you have heard the saying, somewhat over-simplified but still true, 'A happy wife makes a happy life'?"

Sampson nodded slowly.

"Giving to the poor is the exact same concept, just on a broader scale," the wizard continued, "If you ask those who regularly give to the poor why they engage in such an act, they will usually give a terse answer such as 'because the poor need it,' or 'because no one else will help them', or because they want to 'give back.' But, if you press these people for more specifics, they will eventually admit they give to the poor because it makes them feel good, or feel fulfilled, or feel connected. In short, it makes them happy."

"But there are those who give to the poor simply because they feel obligated," Sampson pointed out. The wizard nodded his head sadly.

"Alas, true. There are those souls," the old man said quietly, "but even those people are seeking their own happiness, even if they themselves are unaware of it. If they feel obligated to give to the poor, and they in fact do give, that simply means they would be less unhappy giving than if they did not give. Their anterior reason is different from those who give freely, but their true ulterior reason is the same. Equally as important, these people do not seek happiness. Instead, they seek to *avoid unhappiness*, and that is not the same thing."

"So, you are saying that some people are not fully aware of why they are happy," asked Sampson.

"Unfortunately, yes. But you must not be one of these people. You must fully understand not only what makes you happy, but why these things make you happy. You must also live a life devoted to seeking this happiness, not simply avoiding unhappiness."

"I wish to amass great wealth," said Sampson with a gleam in his eye, "I know that will make me happy."

"You will never amass such wealth," the wizard said bluntly. Sampson gave the old man a shocked glare.

"What?" he asked.

"You believe that wealth will make you happy because you could then purchase things that you are unable to purchase now?"

"Well, yes!" Sampson blurted out.

"Is there any other reason why wealth will make you happy?"

"Not that I can think of."

"Then my statement stands. You will never accomplish this goal."

"Why not?"

"Take up your parchment and write this down."

Sampson was annoyed at the sudden break in the conversation, but he obeyed the old man. Reluctantly, he snatched up the parchment and, following the wizard's instructions, began to write:

Tenet Two

Success in any area requires many different reasons for accomplishment, not just one.

After writing, Sampson stared at the parchment for a moment and regarded the old man once again. The wizard said nothing. He merely sat back in his chair with a small closed-lipped smile on his craggy face. The silence carried continued for several moments, until Sampson could abide no more.

"I am sorry," the young man said, "but this tenet is wrong."

"Really?" the wizard responded with sudden animation, "And why is that, O' learned elder of the ages?"

"Because," Sampson said, "if you have a reason that is powerful enough, a man can accomplish anything."

"There do exist conditions where this is true," the wizard replied, and Sampson was quite surprised that the old man was agreeing with him. "For example, if I asked you to stand up from your chair, you may or may not do it. However, if I offered you a thousand pieces of gold to rise from your seat, then likely you would obey such a request, even though you had only one reason to do so."

"Thank you," Sampson said, nodding smugly.

"But," the wizard continued, "Tenet Two does not refer to quick, simple tasks. It refers to success. And success requires sacrifice and hard work over a long period of time. It requires the completion of many tasks that you will not want to complete. It requires the conquest of your own fears. All of these things are extraordinarily difficult. And most importantly, these arduous duties take time. If you do not have many different compelling reasons to drive you onward, you will eventually cease the uncomfortable and painful work that success in any area requires."

"You are speaking of persistence," interjected Sampson.

"Ah yes," the Archmage muttered, shaking his head slowly, "Persistence has become an almost hallowed word that is praised by many, but what is never mentioned is that persistence does not occur in a vacuum. Persistence does not manifest itself for no reason, nor simply because of great willpower. Willpower exists within the human psyche for short, concentrated periods of great need or emergency. The function of willpower was simply not designed to be utilized over a long period of time. Willpower is a great force when drawn forth in short bursts, but over time, willpower will fail. If you have piles of reasons why you must succeed, your reasons will carry you forward when your willpower dies. And willpower will eventually die. It always does."

"I am trying to find fault in what you have said," Sampson said softly after a long silence, "but I cannot find any. I will think more on this."

"As you should," said the wizard, "but while you are thinking. I would also have you read. On the table behind you are some books that I have chosen. You are to read all of these, cover to cover. Once you have finished, you will be free to choose any other books in my library to read, but only when I am sure that you have read these initial ones."

"Alright," Sampson said, with more than a little excitement. He had always enjoyed reading, and the selection of tomes available in his small village had always been lacking.

"Every morning, starting tomorrow, you shall begin the day with physical exercise. You will run, to improve your heart, your lungs, and the system that carries blood and air through your body. You will also haul granite blocks at the rear of my tower that I need moved. This will improve your muscles and your skeleton. Only after you have done such things will your knowledge work begin."

"What?" cried Sampson, "What value is the work of muscle to the acquisition of knowledge?"

"You will no longer be working hides with your father while you are with me," answered the old man, "and the mind functions only as efficiently as the body that bares it. Many old so-called 'wise men' have forgotten this basic truth, and are victims to debilitation and early death. The teaching you will receive shall do you little good if your brain is slow or your wits are fatigued. And your knowledge will do you little good if you live only a short time to apply it. Do not discount the value of your physical body simply because you were raised in a home where physical work was required often. Now take your books and go. It will take you weeks to read all of them I am sure, so you would do well to begin now. We will meet again tomorrow."

Chapter Three

The next morning, after he had completed his morning exercises, Sampson took advantage of a strange bathtub that he found down the hallway from his room. It would instantly fill with warm water as soon as he touched it. A nice, long bath later, Sampson dressed and met the Archmage in his workshop.

The room was larger than the library, although with a lower ceiling. Beakers, bottles, books, papers, tubes, and containers filled with all kinds of odd and disgusting ingredients were all about the room on tables and shelves. The Archmage was in the center of the room seated at a table, upon which was a strange-looking creature. It stood upright, about three feet in height with an almost shiny black skin, except for its stomach, which was a dirty white. Instead of arms, it had flippers like a great fish. Its tiny black head sported a pointed birdlike beak and its feet were clawed and webbed.

The odd creature made a series of light, high-pitched noises while looking in the wizard's direction, and the old man would occasionally nod or make some other acknowledging gesture.

"Um, hello," said Sampson, worried that he was interrupting something.

Apparently he was, for the wizard and the creature both turned and gave him an annoyed look "Yes, yes," the Archmage said hurriedly, "just sit down. I shall be with you in a moment."

Sampson sat down at a table adjacent to the Archmage and the creature and observed the spectacle.

"Yes, yes," the old man said to the animal, "I do believe you are addressing her needs, but women are emotional creatures. It is not simply the words you say but also how you say them."

The animal made more squeaking noises and bobbed his head up and down.

"Well, thank you," said the Archmage, "and do make sure your children clean up their toys next time."

The creature made a few clicking noises, hopped off the table, and waddled out of the room.

"Now," said the old man turning to Sampson, "where were you and I?"

"Wait a minute! What in the realms was that?" Sampson asked, pointing at the odd beast making its exit.

"A penguin, of course," said the wizard.

"A penguin?"

"Yes. Pygoscelis adeliae, an amphibious bird of the freezing climes," the old man explained, "When I was young, I found them amusing, and I always wished to own one. Now an entire family of them live downstairs in a room that I maintain at a constant freezing temperature."

Sampson shook his head. "I do not think I understand," he said, for there were some odd words in the wizard's speech he did not comprehend.

"Likely you do not," said the wizard, "Nevertheless, you and I must begin."

"First," said Sampson, "tell me of that wonderful bathtub! How does it work, with the magical water it creates?"

"If you fail to understand the penguin's home, you shall surely fail to understand the explanation behind the creation of water."

"No, please, tell me," Sampson prodded.

"Very well," the old man sighed, "it is a matter of molecules."

"Molo…molo," Sampson stuttered.

"Molecules," said the Archmage impatiently, "The magic I imbued into the bathtub combines oxygen molecules with those of hydrogen, thus creating the compound mineral hydrogen oxide, or in layman's terms, water."

"Oh," said Sampson, still trying to wrap his mind around the wizard's odd words. Summoning up something intelligent to say, Sampson added "Uh, I did not know that water was a mineral."

"Well, technically it is only classified as a mineral when it is frozen as ice," said the wizard as if he had been caught telling a fib, "Water is certainly not an element, and ice is most definitely a mineral, such being defined as having a homogenous chemical composition with an organized structure and of a natural inorganic origin."

"Ah," Sampson said, nodding knowingly but not understanding a thing the wizard had just said.

"But enough of birds, bathtubs and chemistry, boy!" the old wizard blustered, "It is time to get down to today's business! Now, I know that you have had some measure of schooling in your life. Otherwise you would scarcely be able to spell your name, much less read and write."

"Yes," said Sampson, "there are several women, scholars who often journey from the city of Maikanna, where the king sits. They teach some of the local children subjects such as mathematics, history and reading. Also, our local priest engages in schooling of the youth as well. I myself learned from both the priest and the scholars, mostly because I enjoy reading."

"You can read, write, and speak well," the old man observed, "but can you add, subtract, multiply, and divide?"

Sampson replied, "Yes, sir."

"And were you ever taught the history of our kingdom? And of the world beyond?"

"Yes. Mostly the history of our own kingdom."

"And of science? Biology, geology, metallurgy, alchemy, and the like?"

"Oh yes! I am learned regarding the different types of animals, the mixtures of alloys like bronze and steel, the movement of the sun around the earth…"

"Let us stop right there," said the old man, "Write this down on a new piece of parchment."

Sampson obeyed, and when he was done he had written:

Tenet Three

Most of what you have been told is wrong.

So bizarre was this statement that Sampson said nothing. He only stared at the old man in compete bewilderment.

"Tell me, boy," the wizard said, seemingly pleased the young man was confused, "you spoke of alloys. Which is the harder, the element of iron or the alloy of bronze?"

"I was taught this!" Sampson said, snapping his fingers, "Iron is of course the harder! After all, many times have I read in tales the phrase 'he a had a grip like iron'. Never have I heard it said, 'he had a grip like bronze'."

"Nevertheless," the wizard said, "it is a falsehood. It is bronze that is harder, not iron. They only spin the tale of iron being harder so that the foot soldiers in the king's army, armed with iron blades, do not feel inferior to the officers in the army, who often carry bronze swords." Sampson blinked several times. He was quite surprised.

"You also spoke of the sun circling the earth," the wizard continued, "tell me of this."

"Of course," said Sampson, "The earth, as everyone knows, is a vast, flat plain, the edges of which are located in the farthest oceans, where the water falls into the great void in which the plain floats. The sun, a small ball of flame, circles 'round the earth once per day, rising from the eastern edge of the world in the morning, and setting below the western rim of the world in the evening."

"Indeed?" said the wizard with mock interest.

"Well, yes," said Sampson, not understanding the wizard's amused expression.

"Allow me to enlighten you on a few minor points," the Archmage began, "The sun does not revolve around the earth, but quite the opposite, the earth revolves around the sun. I shall also tell you that the sun is not a small ball of fire floating in the sky, but a huge furnace of explosions, hotter than the fires of hell itself, and it is so colossal that one million of our earths could fit within and still there would be room to spare. Moreover, the earth is not flat as one of the pancakes your mother prepares for your morning breakfast. Instead, it is spherical, like a bubble. The reason you see the sun 'move' across the sky is not due to the movement of the sun, or even the movement of the earth around the sun, but because of the fact that the earth spins on an axis, like a barn's weather vane during a windstorm, thus creating the illusion that the sun moves about the earth's sky. But by far, the greatest fact in all of this is…" The old man stopped as he saw the expression of complete terror fly across the young man that sat across from him.

"What are you saying?" Sampson cried, "That is pure lunacy! The earth shaped like a…like a ball? The sun a million times larger? Madness!"

"Not a million times larger," the Archmage corrected, "a million times larger in volume only. It is about 190 times the larger in diameter. It is all a matter of how you measure the thing."

Sampson's terror quickly became laughter. "That is crazy!" he squeaked out between chortles, "I am surprised you have not been burned at the stake for heresy by the high priests!"

"Very interesting that you should make such an observation," said the wizard, his eyes narrowing, "for it is because of those very priests that you do not have this information."

"Ha!" Sampson exclaimed, "What shall be my next lesson? Shall I learn from your penguins how to fly underwater? Or how to sing, perhaps?" Sampson flew into another cacophony of laughter.

"Boy," said the wizard, who was not sharing the joke at all, "I have cast bolts of lightning into the skulls of men who have made less insult of me."

Sampson's laughter came to an abrupt halt.

"Because what I have told you is so radical to that which you have been taught, I shall overlook your remarks, but do not ever again forget to whom you speak. I have lived on this earth for the span of many lifetimes and was uncovering the secrets of the universe when your great-great-great-grandfather was only a babe in his mother's arms. What I say is the truth. It only saddens me such that great truths are not passed on to the world's youth." The old man's eyes drifted downward, and he seemed possessed of dark thoughts.

"Even if I were to believe your claims," Sampson said carefully, no longer laughing, "what evidence do you have to support what you have said? Surely you cannot blame me for my skepticism?"

"It is evidence that you require?" the wizard said, coming back to life, "then evidence you will have, though I sincerely hope you did not have a large breakfast."

"What?" Sampson asked, not understanding once again. Instead of responding, the Archmage quietly rose from his seat and flashed his hands about in a complex pattern.

Then the world exploded.

Searing flashes of light bombarded Sampson's eyes, and he slapped his hands to his face in terror. To Sampson's surprise, there was no pain, only shock. His hands were still covering his eyes when he began to realize that his feet were no longer touching the floor. No other part of his body was for that matter.

"Well, open your eyes, boy. You are quite safe," came the old man's voice from nearby. Sampson slowly pulled his hands away and witnessed the panorama that was before him.

The young man stood, or rather floated, for there was no floor or anything else supporting him, within a gigantic dark void of pitch black. Small white stars spotted the void in all directions like stationary snowflakes. Dominating the scene was a huge disk that hovered before him, mostly blue and green in color, but covered in whips of white. The disk was much larger than him and the wizard who stood floating several feet from him. The old man did not seem worried in the least. Rather, he seemed quite content, and drank in the view.

Suddenly, a stabbing yellow light peeked over the upper side of the disk, and Sampson shielded his eyes. He could almost make out a white circular form within the light, though it was too bright to look at directly. Slowly, and quite carefully, Sampson reached out to touch the huge disk that hovered in front of him, but his hand met only air. It wasn't until then that Sampson realized that the disk was actually much larger than it appeared, and was probably very, very far away.

"Magnificent, is it not?" the old man asked. His voice had lost some of its cranky edge to it, and a feeling of relaxation seemed to overcome the wizard.

"What is this place?" was all that Sampson could ask.

"You look upon our world," said the Archmage, "for we are now far above the clouds, hundreds of miles from the ground. We are in the space between worlds and stars, so that you may see our world for what it is, and not what you were told it is. The light ahead is the sun, itself a star, and over in that direction," the wizard pointed in the area opposite the sun, "you can see our moon."

"But, how is it we are here?" Sampson breathed.

"Magic," the Archmage said simply, "of a very complex kind. It took me many a year of study and experimentation to master it. Many variables involved. Not just teleportation, but maintaining our relative movement to the earth, and its axial rotation and travels around the sun, and also our own protection. There is no breathable oxygen in this great void, not to mention the lack of air pressure, and the temperature is deathly cold. Were it not for the invisible sphere in which we drift, you and I would die nigh instantly due to a host of reasons."

It was almost too much for Sampson to grasp.

"This…this is our earth?" Sampson said after a few moments.

"Indeed," replied the Archmage, "And as you can see, it is quite round, though its actual spherical quality is difficult to appreciate from this particular vantage point."

Sampson could hardly believe how matter-of-factly the wizard spoke in the presence of such majesty. The panorama that was splashed before the young man was like nothing he had ever imagined in his most vivid fantasies. After breathing it all in for several more moments, Sampson realized something and turned to the old man.

"You…you are powerful beyond all imagining!" he cried, "These sorcerous powers you wield are beyond the power of the greatest of kings! Are you…are you a god?"

The Archmage laughed, and Sampson realized it was the first time he had seen the old man do so. It was a true laugh, a laugh that rumbled deep from the old man's belly.

"Alas, no," the old man remarked, "Nothing even near it, nor would I ever wish it so. I am only a man, just as you are. Slightly more aged, perhaps."

"No…" Sampson began.

"Yes," said the Archmage, "Listen to me young Sampson, and hear this if you have heard nothing else I have told you. I have not accomplished a single thing that you could not accomplish given time, and I will never accomplish anything that is beyond your abilities, or the abilities of any other. I am simply a man who long ago decided what made him happy, what he wanted, determined how to get what he wanted, and worked hard to achieve it. You could do no worse. It is a monumental blunder to assume that someone who has accomplished something that you have not is a greater person than you. It is always easier to look at someone who has done great deeds and assume that somehow that person is superior to you. The fact is that *there is no greater person than you*. There are only those who have taken the time to accomplish great things, time that you have not yet taken. Will you take the time to accomplish such? Only you can answer this question."

Sampson regarded the old man and looked back over the universe that lay before him. "It just seems all so far beyond me," he said quietly, mostly to himself.

"It always does, in the beginning," the wizard said, just as quietly.

There was a flash of light, and the rush of gravity came suddenly and unbidden to Sampson's body. With a thud, he landed in his seat back in the wizard's laboratory. The wizard was seated before him once gain, a bored expression on his face like nothing unusual had happened.

"We are back," Sampson noted.

"Indeed," said the Archmage, "you did not expect me to keep us out there all day, did you? I, for one, would certainly not enjoy missing lunch."

Sampson's mind was racing with many different conflicting thoughts. They quickly coalesced into one emotion; anger.

"I was never told any of this!" Sampson cried, "I have had schooling for the past twelve years! More than most my age have had! And I have read many books. Not one spoke of these things! You are right! I have not been told the truth."

The old man gave Sampson a shocked look. It was as if the Archmage was actually surprised that, for once, Sampson was not arguing with one of his points.

"It is a conspiracy!" Sampson screamed, "It must be! A conspiracy of the lords, the dukes, and the clergy, and even the king, or perhaps all the rulers of the lands around the world! A conspiracy of kings! To keep the peasantry in line!"

Sampson stopped his rant long enough to note that the wizard was smiling almost in a mocking manner.

"Well," Sampson railed, "what else could it be?"

"First," said the wizard, "you argue my every point. Now, when I bestow upon you a bit of wisdom you actually agree with, you agree with it so much, you take it to a distant extreme. Yes, Tenet Three is most correct. Much of what you have been told by the world is wrong. Much of what you should have been told has been kept secret from you, or has been ignored or forgotten. There are many reasons for this, but some kind of grand world-spanning conspiracy by the elite is not one of them. While there may be some information filtering at the top of society for nefarious reasons, such information has a tendency to slip out. Some people are simply too watchful."

"But why then?" Sampson asked.

"As I said, there are many reasons. You were not told about the difference in iron and bronze so some in the military could save face. You were not told about the shape of the earth so some so-called sages, alchemists and other scientists would not be embarrassed. You were not told about the earth revolving around the sun because of religious dogma. The reasons for incorrect teachings are legion. Embarrassment, political agendas, guilt, anger, religious beliefs, comfort, stupidity, laziness, ignorance, control over others, and resistance to change are but a few. We could spend many an hour discussing the whys, but what is most important is that you know it does happen; that you have been told things that are outright false by many intelligent, experienced, well-meaning people throughout your life. Now you know this. Now you can open your mind to the truths of life."

"Truths?" Sampson asked, his voice much quieter now.

"Truths," said the old man softly, "Some truths are simply interesting, like the bronze and the iron. Others, like your recent adventure in space, are shocking, but not life-changing. Others are truly life altering experiences, if one embraces them."

"Which truths are these?"

"Again, there are many, but I will give what I believe to be the greatest of them all. The root to the tree, if you will. It is the reality that life is not complicated."

"Life is not complicated?" Sampson parroted, "That is the great truth?"

"Indeed, there are greater truths in the universe," the wizard said, "but for you, at this moment, I believe this to be the greatest."

"Then, please explain," Sampson said anxiously. After spending time with the Archmage, much of his original skepticism was rapidly fading.

"Very well," the wizard began, "let us take your basic desire; your yearning for riches. I shall ask you, is your father a wealthy man?"

"No," Sampson said simply, "though I am not sure that he desires to be."

"Are any men in your village flush with coin?"

"Well, I would say no," said Sampson, "though the mayor seems to have a nice home."

"And why are they not wealthy?" the wizard continued, "have you asked them?"

"Oh," Sampson said, "I have asked some, and they have given many reasons. They have said that it is very hard to become wealthy. That you must perform hard, back-breaking work for decades upon decades. That you must be very highly educated and skilled, and that you must be one of the best in the land in your chosen area of expertise. And you must be lucky, they say, since you can work all of your life and still not be able to achieve wealth. And you must be ruthless, they say, since you must be tough on those who work for you and a tough negotiator with other people in the marketplace. It is a great sacrifice to pursue riches, because it takes so much out of you. You will rarely be able to be with your children or your lover or have any time to relax they say, since the desire for wealth will consume your life. It is for all these reasons that the men in my village have chosen not to pursue riches. At least, that is what they have told me."

"My, my," said the old man, "pursuing riches certainly sounds brutal, does it not?"

"Yes," Sampson agreed.

"It sounds somewhat complex, does it not?" the wizard asked again.

"Yes," said Sampson, "the thought of it has even frightened me."

"It certainly sounds like the men in your village are relieved and happy with their lives, since they all chose to not pursue such a life," the wizard observed casually.

Sampson was about to answer, but then stopped himself, glancing at the wizard with a questioning eye. The Archmage smiled sharply, but suddenly changed the subject.

"When a gorgeous person walks by, and people admire the man or woman, they also begin talk of how they could never look like that, because it is simply too hard to keep note of everything they eat or to exercise the proper amount. When someone begins a small business venture, and the venture becomes successful, people talk of how rarely that happens, because it is so hard to be successful in business, it being such a complicated process.

"And such is what these people *must* say about these things. If a man is without a thing he wants, and he sees another man with that thing, it is much easier to say how complicated and difficult it is to receive such a thing, than it is to perform the tasks necessary to receive that thing himself. If everyone actually admitted that staying thin is a simple process, every chubby person would instantly feel ridiculous. But if everyone speaks of how complicated it is to be thin, everyone who has grown fatter would not only feel normal, but validated. The same is true for those who are poor and not wealthy, battling with their lover and not joyous with them, ignorant and not knowledgeable, passive and not powerful, sick and not healthy, or miserable and not happy. People simply speak of complexity and hardship to make themselves feel better, not because these things are actually difficult or complicated. These things may take time and work, but they are not complicated. There is such a desire to feel validated by people's own poor decisions, they directly violate Tenet Four."

Sampson snatched up his notes and rifled through them. "Uh…Tenet Four?" he said, "I do not think you have covered that yet."

"What?" the wizard said sharply. "Great hermit crabs!" he screamed, "You are right! I deserve to be strangled to death with my own beard for such an oversight! Tenet Four is quite possibly the greatest of all Tenets! Drakes and dread!"

"Um, instead of beating yourself up about it, why do you not just give it to me now?" Sampson asked, pen in hand.

"Of course!" said the wizard.

This is what the Archmage recited and Sampson wrote:

Tenet Four

Acknowledge the way the real world works in real life, even if it is unpleasant to do so, regardless of your own biases.

"So," Sampson observed, "By saying these things are hard to accomplish when they are in fact not, these people are not acknowledging the way the real world works in an effort to feel better about the decisions they have already made."

"Decisions they feel little effort to change," the wizard added, "How motivated are you to pursue riches if you believe to do so will create a tedious life? And while you are not pursuing riches, you are simply validating the masses of people who have already told you how hard it is."

"That is well and good," said Sampson, "but are you saying it is easy to become wealthy or to have a body like Hercules? 'Life is easy'…is that what you are saying?"

"First," said the wizard, "it is critical to understand the difference between the word 'easy' and the world 'simple'. These are two very different words. Life is not 'easy'. Not at all. Nor is it 'easy' to achieve success in any area of life…financial, physical, romantic, or any other. No! No indeed. But, it is very 'simple'."

"I do not follow," said Sampson.

"Those large blocks I have you moving every morning…is it a complicated process to move them?"

"No," Sampson grumbled, "it is just tiring."

"But the process is simple."

"Yes."

"Yet, it is also difficult."

"Yes!"

"Therefore, you understand how something can be very simple, but not easy, all at the same time. Such is the process of achievement."

Sampson nodded, and his back began to ache just thinking about the blocks he would have to move tomorrow morning.

"Generating wealth is such," said the wizard, "in order to do so, there are only about five or six simple things one must do on a regular basis, some of which are not easy, but *all* of which are simple. In order to build strong muscles and reduce the amount of fat on your body, there are only five or six simple things you need to do on a regular basis. This goes for everything else one would want to accomplish in life…raising happy children, starting a business, being successful in a trade, being harmonious with a lover. These are very, very simple things to do.

They are not easy, since they require a constant, consistent effort, but they are simple. It is how men come from nothing to become kings. It is how I became an Archmage. It is how you will accomplish what you wish. Do not ever be burdened by the thought of anything being too complex or difficult to accomplish. Nothing truly is. It is a pity that most people find it easier to disparage great deeds than to accomplish them themselves."

"It is simple for me to accomplish wealth and achievement?" Sampson mused. It just didn't sound right.

"It is," said the wizard, "especially if you start with the first three Tenets as your foundation, and maintain Tenet Four throughout your life. You establish that your primary objective is to discover what will make you the happiest in the long term. Then you determine what that is. Your new primary objective is the accomplishment of that goal, even if that goal is considered 'unrealistic' by others. This does not faze you, since you know that much of what you have been told in this area is untrue (Tenet Three). You fortify the goal with many reasons you have for its accomplishment, knowing that your reasons will carry through the upset and adversity that you know must come (Tenet Two). Then, as you set out to accomplish your objective, you are achieving more in one year than many do in ten, since you are constantly operating in the real world, not some feel-good fantasy world that you have constructed for yourself."

"Tell me of that," Sampson said, stopping the old man, "How is it that I may accomplish in one year what many do in ten, because of the 'real world', as you say?"

"The magic I wield is formidable," the Archmage said, "With but a wave of my hand, I could shatter this stone tower we sit within, if I so wished. But, the power of Tenet Four is far greater.

"For example, two men wish desperately to work for the city's master blacksmith as an apprentice, and then some day become a master blacksmith themselves. The first man follows his parent's advice; he gets schooling. He is schooled in many areas of academia, almost none of which have anything to do with blacksmithing. However, the second man is a student of Tenet Four. He does not get any schooling. Instead, he devotes time to working for the local village blacksmith. His friends mock him. His parents are angry with him, for they too wish for him to receive schooling. Because of his sweat and dirt, the pretty girls in the village avoid him.

"Soon, both men go to offer their services to the master blacksmith. The master can only hire one man, and the first man believes himself to be the easy victor. After all, he has schooling! The second man is an ignoramus, barely able to read.

"The master sees one man with much schooling and knowledge but no practical experience in the blacksmith trade, and another man with no schooling but several years of real, actual blacksmithing skill. He chooses the second man almost instantly. The second man becomes a master blacksmith in short order, used by the king himself, and becomes renowned the kingdom over as one of the greatest blacksmiths in recent memory.

"The first man is dumbfounded. He is baffled as to why the ignoramus received the job when he did not. Eventually, he goes back home and tells others how 'difficult' and 'complicated' it is to be a successful blacksmith. Like many others, he settles for mediocrity and eventually fades away into history. The first man does not follow Tenet Four. He does not realize that the world does not operate the way you *want* it to operate. It does not operate the way you *think it should* operate. It does not operate in a manner that you believe to be fair, right or moral. Sometimes, it does not even operate in a way that you believe makes sense! The world operates the way it operates, whether you like it or not, whether it matches your biases or not, and whether you even acknowledge it or not.

"In the real world, you may not like the fact that work experience often trumps schooling, but it does. You may not like the fact that the government officials whom you elect to high office behave in a manner opposite to what you wish, but they will. You may not want to believe that punishing your children will make them happier adults, but it shall. You may believe it wrong that people may judge others based strictly on their appearance, but they will. You may not want to admit that people can amass great wealth very quickly in life when you have not, but they can. You may deem that others will always behave in a selfless and honest manner, but often they will not. You may not want to admit that men marry women who are prettier and women marry men who have more money, but they do. You believe that the act of walking for a few minutes every morning will cause you to lose a large amount of fat, but that alone will not. You may believe that the special person in your life will never leave you because you love them or because you are a good or capable person, but they can at any time.

"You may choose not to acknowledge the way the real world works. You may instead pretend that the world works the way you wish it to because it makes you feel better. But, as I have said, time is the great determiner of all things. If you live your life believing the world is what you want it to be and not what it actually is, you are going to travel a very long, miserable and painful road throughout the days of your life.

"Since most people walk through life thinking the world is the way they want it and not the way it actually is, you, as a follower of Tenet Four, have a titanic advantage over these people. This is how you will literally accomplish in one year what it takes them to accomplish in five, ten, twenty years, or even longer. An extra benefit to you is the primary objective in life, which is happiness. Others who do not follow the real world will be constantly surprised, confounded, angry, depressed and frustrated at every turn. On the other hand, while you might look a little odd to these people at first, you will experience happiness on a massive scale, since you are operating the machine of life the way it was meant to be operated."

Sampson sat back in his chair and breathed deeply. He could sense a real change within his mind and his soul. For the first time in his life, he felt a power within him, as if he could rise from his humble existence, go out into the world, and accomplish whatever he wished. It was almost as if he, Sampson, was becoming a wizard himself.

"Before you go off conquering the universe," the old man scolded, as if reading Sampson's thoughts, "you must know that I expect you to pass on all knowledge that I impart to you onto others. Knowledge is not like a dragon's gold, to be horded away in some deep cavern for hundreds of years. It is to be shared with the world. This is a prime reason for your presence here in my tower."

Sampson shook his head. "By your own admission," the young man began, "most people are not successful, nor have any desire to be. What makes you believe that they would use, much less even want to hear, your knowledge?"

"Drakes and dread!" the wizard cried, slapping his hands on the table, "Assumptions again! You really must work on this!"

"What are you talking about?" Sampson sputtered.

"Is a man who never achieves riches of money throughout his life successful?" the wizard asked.

"Of course not," Sampson replied.

"Really? What if he cares nothing of money? What if his great passion and joy comes from music? From playing the lute and singing for all to hear? What if his motivations come from the happy smiles of the children who hear his song? What if throughout his entire he life plays and sings for all, bringing happiness to all around him, most particularly himself? Is he successful then?"

"Well," Sampson hesitated, "no."

"He is not successful by *your* definition of success!" the wizard bellowed, "but he is quite successful by *his* definition of success! And frankly, such a man would care little for your definition of success indeed!"

"Everyone's concept of success is different," said Sampson, rolling his eyes and waving a dismissive hand, "Yes, yes. So the poor man that lives in a mud hut is successful, as long as he hates money and loves mud."

"As long as he truly loves mud and has no need for money in his heart of hearts," the old man said, with a pointed finger upraised, "As I alluded to earlier, there are many who say things such as 'money is not important. I do not need any,' and these people are simply lying to themselves and others, justifying their laziness or fear, for they really do wish for wealth. But, there are some people in the world who actually, truly, deep down, care little or not at all for money in reality. Other things bring them far more happiness, and thus they are successful if they experience these things often in their lives."

"What difference does this make to me?" Sampson asked, "I know exactly what will make me happy. We spoke of it when we discussed Tenet One."

"Incredible. The arrogance of youth," the old man muttered under his breath.

"What?" Sampson asked.

"I said it goes back to why you must pass on what you will have learned from me," the old man snapped back, "It goes directly to the next Tenet, Tenet Five. Tenet Five describes why all men and women, great and small, successful or not, can benefit from the Nine Tenets of Success and Happiness. It also serves as a motivator when you fail on your way to your objectives. Now write this down!"

And Sampson wrote:

Tenet Five

You are either successful as you define success, or you are unhappy to some degree. There is no third option.

"Everyone," the wizard went on, "and I do mean everyone, must be successful in whatever way embodies success for them, or they will experience unhappiness throughout their life. This will only change when they make the decision to become successful, again, using their personal definition of success, which Tenet One leads them to."

"Tenet Five does sound rather simplistic and sweeping, to the point of generalizing," Sampson noted.

"All the Tenets do, when one first hears them," the old man replied, "but that does not invalidate their wisdom."

"But, are you saying that everyone who is not successful, as they define success, is unhappy all of the time? That is simply not the case. Not in my experience."

"Read Tenet Five once again. It does not say 'miserable all the time'. It clearly says 'unhappy to some degree'. Nor does it state that those who are successful are in a constant state of bliss. Generally speaking, if you wish to do something great with your life, and you never set out to do it, you *will* be unhappy, and quite often too. It is as simple as that. Miserable? Perhaps, perhaps not, but certainly unhappy. You may not even know why you are unhappy, but unhappy you will be. Tell me that unfulfilled people are truly and honestly pleased with their lives. It is simply not so."

Sampson thought for a moment and shrugged.

"A non verbal response," said the old man, "Apparently learning three Tenets in one day has worn your vocal cords. Perhaps now would be a good time to repeat your morning run?"

Sampson frowned, and his legs already started to ache just thinking about it.

Chapter Four

A loud thud awoke Sampson the next morning with a start. After rubbing the weariness from his eyes, he saw the Archmage towering over his bed. He wore a long brown cloak that Sampson had never seen before. His long beard was tucked neatly in his belt, a sight that may have elicited laughter from the young man had he not been so tired. Two large backpacks silently hovered in midair air on either side of the wizard.

"What the-" Sampson began.

He was cut short when the Archmage tapped the floor with the end of the staff he was holding (yet another piece of wizard's regalia that Sampson had not seen until now). Light suddenly filled the room, forcing Sampson to shield his sandy eyes.

"Dress for the road," the wizard said, "today we travel."

"Travel where?" Sampson asked.

"To the site of your next lesson, of course," the wizard came back.

"Could you be a little more specific?" Sampson asked wearily.

"No," the old man said simply, "Now I have already packed food, clothing and other such personals. Come outside when you are dressed. These two bags shall follow you. And do not dally! I will not be having my morning tea this day, and I have a tendency to become somewhat crass when my daily routine is disturbed."

Sampson almost voiced a clever comeback, but decided against it. The wizard was already moving back toward the door and was gone with a swish of his cloak.

Shortly, the two were on the open road. The sun had just risen over the eastern hills, illuminating the peaceful world around them. Rolling green grass surrounded them on both sides, and the air held a crispness that only morning could bring.

The old man was keeping quite a brisk pace, more than Sampson thought a man of his age was capable. The silently obedient backpacks hovered behind both men keeping perfect pace.

"May I ask a question?" Sampson said.

"You just did," the wizard replied.

"May I ask another?"

"You just did."

"Yes, very droll," Sampson said, "I should have seen that one coming."

"Yes," said the old man, staring straight ahead.

"May I ask a question after this one?"

"You may do anything you wish in this world. The question is never whether you may or may not do something. The question is whether or not you are willing to accept the consequences of what it is you do."

"Very well," said Sampson, "Why are we walking to our destination? You are a wizard! Why are we not flying like birds? Or even better, why do we not simply disappear and re-appear at our destination?"

"Ah," the old man said, "I am a wizard, therefore we must travel in strange, mysterious, spectacular ways. Why do we not ride on the back of a great dragon? Or ride in the air upon two winged horses? Or spin our bodies at high velocity and bore through the earth? Would that be more appropriate?"

"You must agree that my question is not a groundless one," Sampson countered.

"Have you not heard the idiom 'Life is a journey, not a destination'?"

"Yes, to the point of tedium."

"Tedious or not, it is quite true. Look about you. Do you not see all you would miss if I were to magically teleport you about? The sweet morning air, the majesty of the mountains in the distance, the call of the gulls overhead, the sun, the sky, the chance meetings of others on the road? One need not be in outer space to witness the splendor of the world. One must instead immerse himself in it."

"You are full of paradoxes," Sampson said, "On my first day you spoke of how important time was, and how foolish it was to waste it. Now, you speak of walking about to witness the world, when flying or teleportation would certainly save precious time."

"Have you heard of Nesharon the Shadowed?"

Sampson was struck by the change in topic, but answered, "Yes, he was an evil sorcerer who destroyed the city of Pescapus years ago with his dark magic."

"Indeed," said the old man, "Alas, there have been many such wizards in history. Too many. But, there are also some like myself. What is the difference between Nesharon and I?"

"Nesharon was an evil man. You are good one, crotchetiness notwithstanding, " Sampson answered.

The old man shook his head softly. "No," he said, "that is far too simple an answer. The difference is that Nesharon was so immersed in his magic that he lost touch with his own humanity, as have all 'evil' wizards. Instead of sipping from the glass of power, they engorged themselves. They ceased to connect with what it is to be human. To be human! Constantly flying and teleporting about is the work of birds and gods, not men. And those men who overindulge in such acts, simply because they are capable of them, cease becoming men. Do you understand?"

"I do," said Sampson nodding, "A strange thing it must be, to have power and yet fear it."

"I fear the power I wield no more than the warrior fears his own sword, than the tavern drinker fears his ale, than the blacksmith fears his furnace. They are all aspects of human existence, yet one must still practice temperance. In all things."

Neither of them spoke to each other for a long time after that, and Sampson tried to take in his surroundings as the old man suggested. Soon, they came across a small village, not unlike the one where Sampson was raised. The sound of water came to Sampson's ears, and he saw a great rushing river to his right. Further down, and well off the road, a large sturdy house sat along a stream that flowed from the river. It was toward this house that the wizard steered.

"Are we going swimming?" Sampson asked with a smile. He was joking, of course, but the thought of tossing off his clothes and jumping in the river was not entirely unpleasant.

"You can dawdle later," the wizard said, "knowledge before amusement. Now pay attention! You are familiar with the preparation of wood for the building of structures are you not? Trees must be felled. Logs must be chopped with axe. Wood must be sawed into boards. It takes many men to accomplish these things, and many do not appreciate the backbreaking work required to raise four walls and a roof about them. There are many millers and woodworkers in this village who are involved in such a profession. It is hard, painful work. All of them callus their hands and sweat their foreheads their entire lives to cut their wood. All but one."

As they approached the home, Sampson detected new sounds by the water. There were creaking sounds, accompanied by an unnatural sloshing.

"One woodman was different," the old man continued, "While all the other woodmen in the village worked very hard, he worked harder. While the other woodmen in the village cut wood, he cut twice as much. When they finished for the day, he toiled further. When they relaxed on the weekends, he researched and studied. When they slept, he was putting hammer to nail in the deep of the night. So diligent was he, others thought him strange. But he continued to labor. It is his home that we approach."

"And so I am here to watch a woodman toil away? To learn the value of hard work?" Sampson asked.

"That would be difficult," the wizard answered with a childlike smile, "since the woodman really does not work anymore."

"I do not understand," said Sampson.

"You shall," said the wizard, "Behold!"

The two of them had rounded the house and were in full view of the source of the strange sounds. There, Sampson beheld one of the strangest and most wonderful sights of his life.

Over the house lay a long square wooden shaft, about two feet in diameter and laying horizontally. In a way that Sampson could not discern, this shaft was somehow connected to the stream, and its waters flowed through it. At the end of the shaft, the water cascaded downward onto a gigantic wheel! Not a wagon-sized wheel, but a monstrous circular thing of iron, its diameter easily the length of two very tall men, one standing on the other's shoulders. The wheel was upright, flush against the outer wall of the home, to which its shaft was attached. The wheel was slowly turning, of course, propelled by the constant flow of the stream's waters caught up in the many paddle-like pockets on the wheel's outer edge.

An intriguing invention, Sampson thought, but to what end? Why have a gigantic, perpetually moving wheel attached to your home? It was then that Sampson recalled the Archmage's story about the woodman, and suddenly Sampson began to comprehend.

He was about to ask the wizard another question, when a man appeared from around the corner of the home. He was tall and very powerfully built, with large arms and a hairy chest that could be seen from the collar of his baggy shirt. His body and his gait reminded Sampson of his own hard-working father, but the man's face indicated something very different. As the man approached, Sampson saw not only his smile, but the man's calm, relaxed eyes. This was not a man who felt the stresses of the world as did most men Sampson knew, his father included.

"Master Archmage!" the man said in a jovial, booming voice, "Welcome! I daresay you are early!"

"Most men in the world are habitually late," the old man answered, "and thus, since being on time would actually surprise you, being early would surprise you no less."

The man smiled again and gave the wizard a quick, agreeing nod. He reached out to Sampson and said, "Nevertheless, welcome again. My name is Clint. The Archmage has told me you are his pupil. You should consider that a high honor, for to my knowledge, this ancient curmudgeon has never taken on a student."

Sampson shook Clint's hand and replied, "My name is Sampson, and I do consider it an honor, sir."

"No need to call me sir," said Clint, "Clint will do fine."

"Very well Clint," said the Archmage, butting in, "please explain to the young man the function and purpose of your water wheel."

"Yes," Sampson added, "it is quite extraordinary."

"Why, thank you," said Clint, "The basics of it are quite simple actually. As you can see, the stream of water is directed from above the wheel against its buckets. A combination of the force of this impact and the weight of the water in the buckets keeps the wheel, and thus its shaft, in constant motion. What you do not see from here, is that the rotating wheel shaft, through gearing, transfers this drive to my home's machinery. The machinery in turn spins circular saws I have designed at very high speeds that cut my lumber."

"That is astonishing!" Sampson cried, "You mean to tell me that this wheel cuts your wood for you?"

Clint gave out a rumbling laugh. "How pleasant that would be!" he cried, "but not quite. I must still guide the wood into position to be sawed, so there is still some work involved."

"But," said the Archmage, "not nearly as much work as other woodmen require to produces the same results. While they are pushing and pulling hand saws all day long, Clint guides wood into his saw machinery powered by his water wheel. Clint can cut seven times the wood other woodman can cut in less than a third the time."

"Is this true?" Sampson asked.

"Well…yes," said Clint modestly, obviously a little embarrassed.

"And," the Archmage added, "Clint only works a few hours per day, and only a few days per week, while the other woodmen toil near-endlessly, all day, six or seven days a week."

Sampson gave the woodman an astonished look, and Clint gave a sheepish, assenting nod.

"But, it was not always thus," the wizard went on, "If you would, good Clint, tell the boy of your work schedule before you perfected the water wheel."

"Well," the woodman began, "It was quite different than it is now, I can assure you. My day usually began at 5:30am. I would arise early, so I could plan out the day before the rise of the sun. My challenge was that, even though I had aspirations to live a life not consumed by work, I still had financial obligations to meet. So, I was very focused in the planning of my time. While other woodmen simply had to cut wood, I had to cut wood as well as invest time for the future where I would not have to cut wood as often.

"At sunrise I, like all other woodmen, proceeded to do the work of woodworking. I did so all day, often until 6pm or later. Then, when other woodmen would retire to their homes for dinner and rest, the next stage of my workday would begin. I would read the writings of other crafters and inventors, studying their ways. I would experiment with my own ideas. I would construct, assemble, and test my own models. I would travel to other towns and cities for advice on my projects.

"It came to the point where my wife grew angry with me. For, while other woodmen of the village would be home with their wives and children, I was working in my shop, traveling abroad, studying, or drawing designs. Other workmen thought me quite daft as well."

"And how does your wife feel about your work life now?" the wizard thought to ask, giving a quick sideways glance to Sampson.

"Oh, her opinion has changed dramatically," laughed Clint, "For now, while other wives are without their husbands all day, most days of the week, I am with my family quite often...far more than any other father in the village, I believe."

"I would wish to see more," said Sampson politely.

"Of course!" bellowed Clint, "Come! I shall show you my shop and introduce you to my family. You must also stay for lunch, for my wife is preparing quite a feast."

"You are most generous," said the Archmage.

"As long as you are not serving roasted penguin for lunch," added Sampson with a smirk.

Several hours later, Sampson and the Archmage were back on the road again, making the leisurely journey back to the wizard's home. Sampson had a grand time at the home and shop of Clint the woodman, and vivid thoughts of wonder danced in his mind.

"I was not even aware that men like Clint even existed," Sampson mused as they walked.

"Indeed?" Archmage answered with a raised bushy eyebrow.

"Yes, indeed. He is a man that thinks like no other."

"He is a man that behaves as no other. That would be more accurate. Many men wish for significance. Few pursue it."

"Is that the lesson then? To pursue significance? To innovate? To create or invent something new?"

"Significance, innovation, creation. These things mean nothing to a person unless that person has applied these concepts to Tenet One and Tenet Two. Once applied, these things are simply subsets of those two important Tenets. No, the lesson was something far simpler, and something closer to the essence of the universe. Do you know what the lesson was?"

"I think I do," said Sampson confidently, "Time, as you have put it, is the essence of the universe."

"It is," said the old man sternly, "at least, in the universe in which human beings inhabit. Of other universes I cannot speak."

"Very well," said Sampson, nodding, "Then the lesson was this: Innovation, creation, thinking critically, and aspiring to lofty goals are all meaningless unless you put in the necessary time and energy, and thus sacrifice into these things. What this means is that, initially, you will be working far harder and more intensely than others will work, even if others seem to be working hard already. Once you put in the 'overtime', if you will, then your goals will come to fruition. Then, you will reap the benefits of those goals, even if those goals include working less hard and less often than others, while still reaping the benefits, financial or otherwise. As a matter of fact, the benefits you reap will be far beyond those things, since the success of one area may positively effect the other areas of your life, as Clint was able to spend more time with his family because of his hard work on the creation of the water wheel."

The Archmage did a strange thing. He stopped in the middle of the road, turned to Sampson and put a hand on the young man's shoulder. As he looked at the young man, Sampson saw for the first time not only wisdom in the aged one's eyes, but warmth as well.

"Sampson," the wizard began, "I have used words such as 'moronic' to describe you. No more shall I use them, for it is not so. Indeed, you are among the most insightful and intelligent young men I have encountered in over a hundred years, and I include wizards, scholars, kings, and knights among that list. Know this - it is easily in your ability to become a man of far greater significance and achievement than Clint, or even myself. If there were more such as you, it would be a far better world, and I would be a happier man."

"Well...thank you, sir," was all Sampson could think to say.

The wizard smiled, nodded, and continued his walk down the road. "You are, of course, absolutely correct in your assessment of today's lesson," he said, "and it is encompassed in Tenet Six."

Sampson noticed that one of the floating backpacks had hovered beside him. The thing opened itself, and out flew Sampson's notes and pen. They hovered in front of his face, and Sampson snatched them out of the air. The wizard told him to begin writing, and this is what Sampson inscribed:

Tenet Six

A few concentrated years of pure work and painful sacrifice will prevent you from toiling for a lifetime.

"The virtue of hard work," Sampson noted.

"Hogwash!" the wizard cried, "There is no virtue in hard work alone! That is where people become confused. So many work intensely their entire lives, accomplishing nothing, only to die as drained beings. Working long, hard hours at any endeavor for decades and decades on end is not virtuous. It is unintelligent at best, reckless at worst. A man or woman who has worked for hours on end, every week, for twenty, thirty or forty years is on a very strange life path, especially if that person has interests, loves and obligations outside of work."

"Like children and a wife?" asked Sampson.

"Like children, lover, spouse, family, physical health and vitality, spirituality, recreation, learning, travel, giving back to the community, making a difference outside of one's own tiny little world, and a host of other things that I could name that have very little to do with work. All these things become decayed in one's life because people believe in the idiotic myth of 'hard work'. No, for hard work to be intelligent, it must be concentrated and focused for a few solid years to achieve a specific result. Once the result is achieved, often hard work simply is not necessary, unless you choose to continue despite this fact. But then, you are working because you choose to, not because it is required of you."

"Is that why someone would do this? To work less? How does one know what to do during this focused period?" Sampson asked.

"One knows why he must do this because of Tenets One, Two, and Five. But, as to what to do, one is guided by Tenets Three and Four to the next Tenet, Tenet Seven."

"And Tenet Seven is?"

"Tell me. Now that Clint has perfected his system of income with little work in his village, who then becomes the most intelligent person in Clint's village?"

Sampson thought that to be another of the wizard's stupid questions. "Well, Clint is, of course!" he replied.

"Nay," said the wizard, "it is the man who copies Clint's water wheel concept, and put it into work in his own life."

Sampson frowned.

"Think of it," the Archmage went on, "while Clint spent many long years working tirelessly to achieve his dream of the water wheel, the next man who implements his idea will accomplish the same as Clint in only a matter of months. This man will not receive any less reward than Clint! While Clint is an extraordinary man, it is the truly intelligent man who does not 're-invent the wheel', pun intended. Why pour years of effort into something that someone else has already accomplished? You must realize that anything you wish to accomplish has already been accomplished by someone else. The unintelligent creative person proceeds to start from scratch on accomplishing his objectives, but the intelligent creative person simply finds who has already accomplished what he wishes, and then emulates this person."

"Is there not anything wrong with copying someone in that way?" Sampson asked.

"You must remember Tenet Three," said the wizard, "You have been taught your whole life that pointless hard work is honorable, and that copying others is evil. Both are quite untrue. Copying one's actions, unless the specific act of emulation is illegal, is a clever thing, not a wicked one. If Clint's village soon has ten woodworkers using the water wheel (as I am sure it soon will), *all* in the village are served, and served greatly. In fact, as time goes on and word spreads it will likely benefit the entire kingdom, then perhaps all of humanity. It is simply a group of people following Tenet One. Pursuing your true happiness benefits not just you, but all around you. And because of Tenet Five, these woodmen should follow Clint's example. They are fools if they do not. Write this down then."

And Sampson wrote:

Tenet Seven

Emulate those who were successful before you, but be careful whom you choose.

"What do you mean, 'be careful whom you choose'?" Sampson asked.

"Simple," the old man answered, "Why do you not wish to follow in the footsteps of your father?"

"It would be a violation of Tenet One," Sampson replied, "I do not wish to be a leatherworker."

"And what if your father, as a leatherworker, was a very rich man? Would you then follow him into the leather trade?"

Sampson thought for a moment and then said, "No, I still would not. It is just not compatible with the goals I have set for myself."

"Exactly!" said the wizard, "And Tenet Seven is aware of this. You have spoken of all the men in your village who are miserable because they simply followed the work of their fathers, even if their fathers were very successful in their trades. They indeed followed Tenet Seven, but only the first half. They emulated one more successful than themselves, but they did not carefully evaluate the life of the men they were imitating. You will bring into your life both the good *and* the evil of one you are emulating, so you must make absolutely sure that their disagreeable aspects are acceptable to you. For all have some disagreeable aspects to their lives, no matter how successful or happy. It is simply a matter of degree."

"You must be aware that I cannot copy anyone I wish," Sampson said, "There are some cases where it would simply be impossible."

"Alas, this is true," said the wizard, nodding, "It is true that you cannot exactly duplicate the life of a prince who was born into wealth if your father is not a king. And, seducing the local baron with your exquisite feminine attributes and thus becoming his wife would be quite difficult if you were a man. However, if you diligently research the people whom you wish to emulate before you do so, you will discover these impossible cases. You have two choices then - either you can discard these possible cases and see new ones, or you can start all the way back to Tenet One and revise your objectives. I would recommend the former, for obvious reasons.

"The point of all this is to ensure that you do not simply 'fall in love' too quickly with one particular person or group of people that seem to possess qualities you admire. More research is in order. You must not make decisions on emotions alone. There are many in the world that make decisions with the heart, and then use the mind to reinforce, justify, and defend those decisions. That is like using a hammer to chop wood and an axe to pound nails. The heart is a mighty thing, but its purpose is to empower, to feel, to experience, not to think. That is the role of the mind. Once you have completed Tenet One and you know what it is that you want, use your mind to make the proper decisions. Research. Compile. Analyze. Anticipate. Then make your decision. Then, and only then, use your heart to drive you forward, to risk, to persevere, to overcome, to conquer fear and to stay focused. Then finally to bask in your accomplishments, both large and small. Now, you are using the correct tools for the correct jobs."

The two spoke a little while longer, and soon Sampson fell into deep thought as they walked along. The sun was plunging into the western hills by the time they arrived back at the tower.

Chapter Five

"Today, we go to war!" the Archmage announced.

Sampson almost spewed the oatmeal that he had in his mouth. It had been two weeks since their visit to Clint's, and the wizard's study demands on the young man had increased since then. It was almost as if Sampson had achieved a new level in his education with the wizard. The young man was having a quiet breakfast when the wizard had appeared out of nowhere and began screaming excitedly.

"You and I are to fight?" Sampson asked after swallowing.

"Of course not!" the wizard thundered, "War, by definition, is a conflict between nations, not individuals."

"Our kingdom is not at war, at least not yet," Sampson noted, "is it?"

"No," said the old man, "But alas, there are other lands that are. Today, we go to witness a great battle in one such war, far across the world. Prepare yourself!"

Sampson thought back to his father's sword that they would occasionally practice with. Sampson had always wanted to spend more time mastering the weapon, but the leatherwork had ever taken precedence.

"Am I to fight?" Sampson asked, "My father's sword is back at the village, and I have no armor to speak of." Surprisingly Sampson was more excited than frightened, but going into a war with nothing but his tunic and trousers did concern him.

The Archmage rolled his eyes. "Boy," the wizard groaned, "do you honestly believe that I would expend such time and effort as I have to train you in the arts of the world only to watch as your head is lopped off by some axe-wielding hobgoblin? Nay! We go to observe and to learn, not to do battle."

Sampson gave a sigh of relief. He did notice though, deep within him, a slight sense of disappointment at not being able to wield a mighty weapon against foul foes.

"Go to your room and dress warmly, for the weather of this far land is a bit colder than you are accustomed," the wizard advised.

Sampson quickly shoved another spoonful of oatmeal in his mouth and dashed off to his room.

Dense clouds covered the sky and sharp winds ripped through the air, blowing the tall grass about like angry, grasping fingers. Atop a small hill, there was a brief flash of white light, and Sampson and the wizard stood where moments before, there was nothing. Sampson noted that the wizard had opted for teleportation on this particular trip due to the distance involved. He had momentarily considered asking the Archmage about it, but considering their last conversation regarding the wizard's various modes of travel, he thought better of it.

He pulled his cloak tightly about him and looked over the vast plain before them. Two immense armies squared off against each other. A distance of three hundred footsteps separated them, and they faced each other with grim resolve. One army, the larger of the two, consisted of tall men with square jaws, dark hair and dark eyes. They were well armored and Sampson could tell, even from this distance, that their swords glowed with a pale yellow light. The other army was much smaller, perhaps half the size of the other. While some men of this group sported shiny armor, many were protected either by leather jerkins or by normal clothing alone. Instead of glowing swords, these men had a variety of weapons.

Some had swords, others axes, and yet others spears or halberds of various make and quality. The look of the men themselves was also quite different. While the men of the larger army appeared as proud but grim knights, the men of the other multitude were shorter in stature, quicker in their movements, and shiftier in their eyes.

"Before you," the wizard announced, "arrayed is the army of the Merchant King of Jeslam and the soldiers of the Realm of Samaskac. The Merchant King holds the smaller of the two armies. For ten months now, these two lands have been at war, but it is this battle that shall determine the ultimate outcome."

"The forces of Jeslam are going to be slaughtered," Sampson remarked, "This shall be a quick fight."

The Archmage nodded, "The Firelord of Samaskac and his men are indeed mighty, and fearless in battle, but the Merchant King of Jeslam is shrewd and cunning. Watch, and we shall see who shall win the day."

Sampson watched as rows of horsemen from the Samaskac throng charged the smaller force. Their lances glowed yellow like the swords of their compatriots, and they screamed fell war cries as they drove forward. The smaller army of Jeslam had no horses. They clutched their weapons and awaited their doom. Just before the horsemen slammed into the awaiting army, Sampson noted that the glow from their lances faded and vanished. The smaller army, instead of attacking the horsemen, parted in the middle, forcing the bulk of the cavalry to pour into the center of the host. Then, the surrounding smaller army pounded the horsemen in perfect unison, and Sampson saw many men on both sides meet their deaths. In moments, the ragtag force had defeated the horsemen, leaving only a few riders left alive, feeling the field or surrendering while screaming for mercy.

It wasn't over. The throng of fighting men from Jeslam took up their war cries and charged the remaining force from Samaskac. Unfazed, mailed archers from the larger army launched thousands of arrows high into the air to intercept their attackers. However, because of the mighty winds that swept the area, most of the arrows where blown short of their targets, and much fewer men of Jeslam died than was intended.

Just seconds before the screaming Jeslam men met their armored enemies, Sampson noticed once again the light of their swords fade and vanish. Sampson could almost see the warriors' looks of bewilderment and terror as the light dwindled from their weapons. Then, the men of Jeslam were upon them, and the battle was fierce. The men of Samaskac were brave and skilled indeed, but the loss of their cavalry and their ineffective archers seemed to dampen their fighting spirit.

While the men of Samaskac fought like mighty bears, the men of Jeslam fought like clever cats, always maneuvering, dodging often, and striking quickly. Men from both sides were slain in heaps. Sampson was shocked when the men at the rear of the silver army began to retreat, more men of Jeslam sprang out of the grass, seemingly out of nowhere, to engage their enemies.

"Hidden burrows in the very ground," the Archmage noted, "Crafty."

In short order, though their losses were extreme and few remained standing, the men of Jeslam had won the day. The soldiers of Samaskac who still had their lives had either retreated or surrendered.

"Such a battle," Sampson said sadly, "Yet I had not anticipated such an outcome. You were right when you said the King of Jeslam was a clever man."

"Or an audacious man," said the wizard, "Or simply a prepared man. Many words one could use to describe him. He risked much for this battle. But risk he did."

"And what lesson am I to learn from this?" Sampson asked, "That skill and shrewdness shall overcome superior brute force?"

"War is brutal and joyless, but one can learn much from war, and there are many diverse lessons one could learn from this battle, but I have shown you this to illustrate Tenet Eight. It, like Tenet Seven, has two parts, one obvious, the other far less so."

"I am listening."

"Would you say the King of Jeslam risked in taking on this battle?"

"Yes. Indeed he did."

"The issue then, is one of risk. Without risk, greatness in any endeavor is simply not possible. The universe in which we inhabit is a perfectly balanced affair of positive and negative. It will not reward one who does not risk loss. Safety and security will never, ever, yield valuable results beyond the mediocre. Risk is inherent in a life of meaning."

"Unless one sets very simple goals," Sampson challenged, "A man who follows Tenet One and has consciously chosen to desire only to live in a simple home, put food on the table and nothing more surely does not need to risk anything to meet his needs."

"True," said the old man, "Such a man would be following Tenet One, but would be ignoring Tenet Five. Such a man would not live a life of joy and happiness, only a life of tedium, obligation and boredom. Not risking means not achieving, and Tenet Five tells us that not achieving means sadness and disquiet in one's life."

"So I must risk to be happy?"

"Truly happy, happy in the long term, yes. You do not need to risk often, or risk recklessly, but risk you must. Additionally, risk is the only way one can achieve independence in any area, from the building of a new nation, to the creation of a new enterprise, to simply growing up and moving out on one's own."

"You assume that everyone desires independence."

"Ah," said the wizard, raising a finger and smiling, "you introduce a very interesting argument, one that is often made. One thing I have discovered over my long years is that unhappiness and dependence are inexorably linked hand in hand. When one's dependence on others grows, his misery shall also grow, and the reverse is true as well. I know many young people who are discontented with having to obey the rules of their parents. Concurrently, I know many elderly folk who are financially dependent on others, be it their grown children, the church, or governments, to make ends meet. These are not happy people. Examine any society and find the happiest people. Who are they? They are always those who have achieved their own independence, be it financial independence, emotional independence, freedom of action, or freedom of thought. It is never those dependent on others for these things. To achieve and maintain your own long term happiness, independence must be gleaned from the efforts in your life. The only time you relinquish your independence is when such loss brings a greater gain, and even then you must be careful, hesitant, and rationally selfish when doing so. Your independence is more precious than solid gold, and you must treat it as such."

"I already know all about independence, and I shall never surrender it to anyone, ever!" Sampson cried.

"Than you obviously never intend on marrying," the old man groaned.

Sampson blinked.

"The world is not black and white," the wizard continued, "as much as those such as you and I would wish it to be. As I alluded to, there are times when you may wish to give up some of your independence for a greater good. It is such when you partner with others when performing a task. It is the same when you have children. It is the same when you delegate tasks to others. In each case, you are exchanging bits and pieces of your independence for some greater result. There is nothing wrong with this, provided you have researched your options carefully, parting with your independence prudently, always pursuing your own long term happiness, and always obeying Tenet Four."

"Yes," said Sampson, "This is what they mean when they speak of interdependence."

"Take care," said the wizard gravely, "Interdependence, while slightly superior, is still dependence. You are still dependent on others when in a state of interdependence. Just because these other parties are dependent on you, still does not mean you are free. Many speak of interdependence as the new way, the way of the future world, but in many cases it is still just an excuse for more dependence. Whether trading your independence for dependence or interdependence, be wary, and do not do so lightly, if at all."

"But, even in those situations I still risk much."

"Indeed! Which is why even though you must risk, you do not risk recklessly. Many assume that risk is dangerous, but it is only dangerous if one risks without research and preparation beforehand. Does a man who ventures forth to slay a dragon risk?"

"Of course he does!"

"What if the same man, before entering the dragon's lair, spends three years researching dragons, both in the library in and in the wild, in search of weaknesses, learning tactics which other men have used to successfully slay dragons, as well as other methods of hunting dangerous animals? What if that man employs a mighty wizard to forge a weapon of magic specifically designed to kill dragons and arms himself thus? And, what if he spends several weeks secretly watching this particular dragon from afar, taking note of the beast's size, strength, behaviors, patterns, desires and fears, and makes copious notes which he then studies? What if he arrays himself with a sorcerous cloak that resists fire from a dragon's breath? What if he then takes twenty of the most valiant and mighty knights he can find, arms them with similar dragon-slaying weapons and takes them into the dragon's lair with him after all of his preparation? Does he risk then?"

"Well, yes," Sampson replied, "but he would have such a high probability of success, the risk would be greatly reduced."

"Exactly!" the old man cried, "Risk does not need to be dangerous at all! Risk is only dangerous when one risks without the proper time invested in preparation of risky action. People often shun risk because they assume, incorrectly, that risk must be hazardous. 'I could never start my own business', they say, 'I may lose my life's savings'. They would only be in danger of losing their life savings if they started a business without taking the necessary research and preparation time to ensure the highest probability of succeeding in their venture.

"The King of Jeslam spent several weeks examining the magic weapons that are in use by the Kingdom of Samaskac. He had several wizards develop a counter-spell that would negate the magic powers in the weapons of his enemies whenever the king wished. Then, through several clever manipulations, he managed to ensure that the final great battle between the two armies would take place here, on this field, and even on this day. He knew the winds would be great and positioned his army accordingly, knowing that the forces of Samaskac would use archers. He also sent out scouts days before to find and create hidden burrows where troops could hide until called upon. The overconfident Lord of Samaskac, smug in his superior numbers, did very little to prepare for the battle other than what is routine for such campaigns. Did the King of Jeslam risk? Certainly. But, how much danger was he truly in? Guarantees in risk are impossible, but increasing the probabilities of a positive outcome is really quite simple once effort and time are applied."

"Is that then the second half of Tenet Eight?" Sampson asked coyly.

"It is indeed," said the wizard, and here is what he had Sampson scribe, right there on the hill:

Tenet Eight

Risk is mandatory for success, but only after doing everything possible to put the odds in your favor before the attempt.

"I see a problem here," Sampson noted, "I could theoretically spend a great deal of time preparing before I risk. Years, in fact. Like an old sage, all research and no action."

The Archmage raised an eyebrow, and Sampson's notes floated upwards, out of his hands and into the air. Once hovering in front of his face, his notes started fluttering around his head in circles like a flock of angry crows.

"What have you in these notes?" the old man scowled, "Letters of sappy love to your sweetheart back in your village? Recipes for raisin and fig muffins?"

Sampson snatched his notes out of the air and shoved them under his arm. "You know full well what is in these notes!" he cried, "It is everything I have learned so far!"

"Then I suggest you re-read them at your first opportunity. Perhaps a second reading will allow the words to penetrate your thick skull!"

"I am going to take a guess here," Sampson said smugly, "in that there is something in my question you do not approve of."

The wizards eyes rolled skywards. "Young professor," the old man began, "your questions speak as if there is only one Tenet, the current one we are discussing. There are in fact eight you have learned, with one more to be revealed. These Tenets are powerful individually, but combined into a single movement, they can create miracles.

"You speak of one who spends too much time preparing, researching, and the like, before taking action. Recall Tenet Four! If you are preparing for a thing, you are not accomplishing a thing, therefore you are not truly accomplishing your goal. Yes, you must prepare, but then you must act. Recall Tenet Five! If you are not achieving that which you desire, you will not be happy, regardless of how learned you are on the subject. Eternal learning without action is simply procrastination or fear. It is also a direct violation of Tenet Six. When this Tenet speaks of 'work' it is not referring to preparation! It is referring to *action*!

"And why would one be spending so much time preparing instead of acting? Likely, it is because they are not following Tenet Two! Their reasons are neither numerous nor compelling enough. If they were, procrastination would not be a challenge. There is good reason why Tenet Two is the second of all Tenets. It prevents much unhappiness."

"Very well," said Sampson, "but right now I would like to follow Tenet Four and acknowledge that it is freezing cold out here, and I think it might be time for us to teleport back to the tower."

The old man glowered down at the boy. "Where was I when you became the new Archmage and I the student?"

"Are you seriously not cold?" Sampson asked in amazement.

"Actually, I am quite comfortable," the old man replied, turning to stare off into the horizon.

Sampson clasped his arms together and thought miserably about how the wizard probably had some warmth spell cast over himself and had neglected to do so on Sampson. The old man probably wanted Sampson to be uncomfortably cold, just to teach another crazy lesson.

"I simply dress warmly," said the old man suddenly, "and my truly 'crazy' lessons have yet to begin."

Chapter Six

Sampson grumbled to himself as he approached the granite blocks behind the Archmage's tower. He knew these blocks all too well. He had been moving them as part of the wizard's chores for weeks now. Sampson had determined, long ago, that the Archmage could simply move the blocks with magic with but a wave of his fingers, and was thus forcing Sampson to move them for some other reason known only to the wizard.

It was not all bad, however. A few mornings ago, Sampson had scratched an itch on his shoulder and was surprised to find a hardened muscle where there was naught before. He had dashed to his mirror and examined his body while shirtless. Indeed, a visual examination and a little finger probing revealed there were new hardened muscles all over his body that he had not noticed before.

His thoughts of posing shirtless in front of the girls back in his village were suddenly shattered by a flash of light beside him.

"Arrgh!" Sampson cried, "I really wish you did not do that!"

"And I wish you did not stink so," said the Archmage, "but life is never one hundred percent as we wish it. Only through clarity, rationality, and hard work can we make it ninety, or perhaps ninety-five percent perfect."

"I would settle for one percent perfect if I could take the morning off from moving these blocks!"

"Very well. Today, you shall have the morning off."

"What?" Sampson was shocked. The old wizard was never this nice.

"Indeed," said the old man with a wry smile, "today we take to the road again."

"Where this time?" Sampson asked, suddenly interested.

"Tell me, have you been to the land of Quith?"

"No," Sampson said, a little embarrassed. Although Quith was but a day's travel south from his village, he had never been there. He hated when his lack of worldliness was exposed, especially to the Archmage.

"Then it is time we rectify that. We leave in fifteen minutes. Make ready. And do hurry up!"

Soon the two of them were on the road once again, this time headed south rather than eastward, where Clint's village lay. The two backpacks hovered after them as usual.

"Your independent evening studies have been more focused of late," the wizard said, "What is it you are working on?"

"Wealth acquisition," said Sampson, and the old man could almost see the gold in the youth's eyes, "with wealth, all other things are possible!"

"Are they?" the Archmage asked, "Can a wealthy man live forever? Can he avoid sickness? What if he loses his wealth, as has been known to happen? What then becomes of his happiness?"

"Are you saying wealth is not a worthy goal?"

"Drakes and dread, of course not! Wealth is a key component of happiness. Wealth creates far more happiness than the lack of it. Of course you should strive for wealth! But, striving for nothing *but* wealth is a path to eventual darkness. Too many men and women have been consumed by the love of wealth above all other priorities.

"True, long term happiness cannot come from just one thing, it must come from a short list of several things. Human beings are multifaceted creatures. They have minds, hearts, bodies, and souls. There does not exist one singular thing that nourishes all four of those things. Therefore, all four must be addressed, and addressed often."

"Surely a massive amount of wealth does well for all of those things," interjected Sampson.

"Only to a degree, and not all in equal measure," said the wizard, "Wealth is good for the mind, no question, but wealth will not invigorate your body if you spend all your days sitting at a desk. Nor will it create strong, long lasting relationships with the woman you take as lover or wife. Nor will it raise proper children. Nor will it enrich the spiritual connection you have with the universe. Certainly, if you live your life congruent with Tenet One, Three and Four, wealth will not harm these things, but it will not be enough.

"Proper time must be given to the heart, to create and maintain enriched relationships with others, and the body through proper food and drink and labor, and the spirit with solitude, peace, mediation, and reading. These things are of equal importance to wealth, at least to those seeking true happiness."

"Surely one could over-focus on those areas as well."

"Indeed, and such a man would be in violation of Tenet Nine just as you would be if you spent your life doing nothing but pursuing wealth. Devoting one's life to pursuing nothing but the love of a woman, or a herculean body, or a strong spiritual tie to the world, all of these paths are equally divergent to the path of long term happiness."

"Tenet Nine?"

"Indeed."

"And that is?"

"I shall show you rather than tell you. Behold!"

As they spoke they crested a small ridge, the border to the land of Quith. It was a place of myth and legend that Sampson had heard stories of as a child, though in truth, he had always been frightened to visit such a realm.

All fear vanished from him and was replaced with wonderment. Before the two of them spread a vast grassy plain that stretched flat, all the way to the blue horizon. Spread throughout the plain were several majestic mountains. These were not normal mountains. They were inverted, completely upside-down. The tips of the mountains were buried deep beneath the earth, and each mountain rose into the sky in the shape of a **V**. At the top, the inverted mountains were widest, their massive bases like islands in the sky.

Sampson couldn't decide if the impossible sight before him was more amazing than the vista he beheld from space a few weeks earlier.

"How...how is this possible?" he breathed.

"They are mountains," said the wizard, "They are formed naturally. of course."

"But they are upside-down!" Sampson cried.

"They are indeed," said the wizard, seemingly unimpressed.

"Surely that is not a natural formation!"

"No. Originally the mountains were formed naturally, of course. Several hundred years ago the Mystic Seven, an order of powerful wizards, transplanted the mountains, inverted them, and laid them here, as part of an experiment to expand usable landmass. Their plan was to create cities atop of the mountains, while leaving the plains untouched. They ultimately failed, but the inverting of the mountains succeeded quite well, as you can clearly see."

"But...how do they stay aloft? Why do they not just fall over? Or simply crumble downward?"

"Balance," said the wizard, "They obey Tenet Nine, which I shall impart to you now."

Hesitantly, Sampson pulled his eyes from the majesty before him and withdrew his notes from his floating backpack. He wrote:

Tenet Nine

If you do not routinely address all key areas of your life, your most important area will cease to bring you happiness.

"Tenet One is perhaps the greatest of all the Tenets," said the Archmage, "but it has one possible flaw, a flaw that Tenet Nine addresses."

"Allow me to guess what this is!" Sampson said excitedly.

"Very well," said the old man.

"Well," Sampson began, "those who follow Tenet One are likely thinking of that 'one thing' that will make them happy. That 'one thing' they have always wanted. So when people follow Tenet One, they will likely fall into the trap of establishing one primary thing to pursue in their lives in order to make them happy, much as I am doing with my desire for riches and wealth."

Sampson looked at the old man. The wizard simply stood there staring back at him.

"And?" the wizard asked.

"Well," Sampson continued, "they will then pursue that 'one thing' but will neglect the other areas in their lives that are equally important. This means that either they will never accomplish that one thing, or they will, but the other areas in their lives will be severely diminished. Thus, they will be able to achieve some level of happiness, but not the true long term happiness that you speak of."

"Marvelous!" cried the Archmage, "Exactly correct! The greatest goal you possess cannot bring you all the happiness you seek if the other areas of your life are never addressed properly. Consider the rich man who is sickly, the beautiful woman who is depressed, the muscular man who is poor, the hard-working man who has children who despise him, and on and on. People often forget that happiness cannot come from just one good thing. It comes from a balance of several good things. You have indeed earned your reward this day!"

"Reward?" Sampson asked.

"Come," said the old man, and he strode down the ridge towards the inverted mountains. Sampson was dying to press for more information, but he knew well that doing so would get him no where. So, he silently followed as he desperately tried to control his curiosity.

Soon, the two of them were striding across the plain. Sampson saw that the Archmage was clearly heading for the largest mountain in sight, a huge black monstrosity that blotted out the sun and towered over them. Sampson felt a strange sense of vertigo as the edge of the base of the mountain, thousands of feet above them, slowly passed over them as they moved ever closer. Horrible visions of the mountain choosing this very moment to topple over and crush them both filled the young man's mind.

"We make for the bottom of the mountain," the Archmage said as he walked, "or the top, as the case may be." The old man chuckled to himself quietly, though it did nothing to alleviate Sampson's growing apprehension.

The landscape became rockier and dirt-ridden as they approached the wall of rock and earth before them. Suddenly the Archmage stopped.

"I shall go no further," he said, "You must continue, to that point." He pointed directly to the base of the mountain that began before them. Sampson followed the gesture and thought he saw the glint of something shiny in the earth.

"Go, and return quickly," the old man ordered, "I will wait here."

"Go and do what?" Sampson asked.

"Go, and take what is yours," said the old man, "In life, you must seize opportunities when they present themselves, and make them your own."

Sampson knew from painful experience that was all he was going to receive from the old wizard. So, he sighed and moved forward, although slowly and cautiously.

He navigated the dirt and rocks for about ten minutes, always following the glint ahead. As he closed in, he saw the shape of the shiny object. It was the golden hilt of a sword, embedded diagonally down into the deep earth of the ancient mountain. Wide-eyed and wide-mouthed, he approached and got a better look. Solid gold it seemed, with sapphires, rubies, and diamonds adorning the guard and pommel. For some reason he did not understand, not one speck of dirt or rust blighted its surface.

For a few minutes he stood staring at it, nervous to do anything more. Then, remembering the words of the Archmage, he gritted his teeth, wrapped his hand around the hilt, and pulled.

He had expected the sword not to move, or at least barely move, requiring a great amount of effort to remove from the ground. Instead, the sword silently pulled free from the mountain as easily as from a silk sheath. Its shiny blade was as spotless as the hilt, and Sampson could feel a great power within the weapon.

He sliced the air with it, almost hearing a faint hum as he did so. Or perhaps it was only his excitement or imagination. Such a magnificent weapon this sword was, more beautiful than any sword he had seen in his life, including even those he had seen sported by royal knights.

He gripped it with both hands, concentrating on it, beholding it, loving it. It was indeed *his*.

The Archmage was standing like an old bent tree when Sampson returned to him. The wizard glanced at the magnificent sword in the young man's hands, and smiled.

"Thank you," Sampson said. He did not know what else to say.

"It is not a gift," said the wizard, "nor is it mine to give. You earned it, and you will do still more in the future to continue to earn it."

Sampson said nothing, only looked at the sword once more.

"Now, you will need to learn how to use it!" the old man said.

"You will teach me swordplay? Combat?" Sampson was so excited he could barely contain himself.

"Drakes and dread! Do I look like a knight? Do you see me wearing armor or a helmet or riding a horse? I am a wizard, not a warrior. The martial arts I cannot teach you. That, you must learn from another. Tenet Nine dictates that while the knowledge I can impart to you is important, it is only part of the knowledge you require. You have more things to learn from me, young Sampson, and once done you will learn still more from others, for learning never ceases for those who seek a happy life.

"Soon, our business will be concluded, and your real journey begins, your journey into *action*, to create the life you have planned in your mind. Without action, nothing I have taught you will serve you. Your journey is just beginning."

Sampson turned away slowly and looked out over the world. And the world beckoned him onward.

Sampson went on to learn many things and have many adventures both heroic and tragic. Soon, he became a great wizard and warrior himself, bestowing wisdom to others, while ruling his kingdom from his castle by a golden sea...

...but that is another story...

The Nine Tenets of Success and Happiness

Tenet One

Your primary objective is to accomplish that which will make you the happiest in the long term. If you are unaware of what this is, find out.

Tenet Two

Success in any area requires many different reasons for accomplishment, not just one.

Tenet Three

Most of what you have been told is wrong.

Tenet Four

Acknowledge the way the real world works in real life, even if it is unpleasant to do so, regardless of your own biases.

Tenet Five

You are either successful as you define success, or you are unhappy to some degree. There is no third option.

Tenet Six

A few concentrated years of pure work and painful sacrifice will prevent you from toiling for a lifetime.

Tenet Seven

Emulate those who were successful before you, but be careful whom you choose.

Tenet Eight

Risk is mandatory for success, but only after doing everything possible to put the odds in your favor before the attempt.

Tenet Nine

If you do not routinely address all key areas of your life, your most important area will cease to bring you happiness.

About The Author

Caleb Jones has three careers. His first is as a time management and business consultant, author, and speaker. His second is as a lifestyle design expert for men. He also runs a technology marketing firm.

At age 18 he was working for the seventh-largest software company in the world, the youngest person in a company of 400 employees. At age 19 he purchased his first piece of real estate and became a part-time real estate investor. At age at age 24, Caleb started his own IT consulting firm and reached the top 5% of his industry's earning level within three years. He has since worked with over 300 companies of all sizes including the Fortune 500, all over the United States, Europe and Asia. Caleb's business articles have appeared in national publications such as National Public Accountant, Medical Economics Magazine, and many others. Caleb has spoken to numerous audiences on the topics of time management, productivity, technology, business success, dating, and relationships. He runs several blogs which receive millions of page views per year.

Caleb lives in the beautiful Pacific Northwest USA, loves the outdoors, and travels frequently. He has two children.

For more information on how Caleb can help you achieve your goals, go to www.calebjones.com.

www.ingramcontent.com/pod-product-compliance
Lightning Source LLC
Chambersburg PA
CBHW030448300426
44112CB00009B/1219